Original title:
The House of Forgotten Echoes

Copyright © 2025 Creative Arts Management OÜ
All rights reserved.

Author: Tobias Sterling
ISBN HARDBACK: 978-1-80587-092-0
ISBN PAPERBACK: 978-1-80587-562-8

Where Silence Breeds Remembrance

In corners lurk old shoes, all worn,
Untied laces, slightly torn.
They whisper tales of dancing feet,
While dust bunnies roll, moving discreet.

A cat once sat upon a chair,
Pretending not to have a care.
But echoes of her purring play,
As laughter rolls the night away.

Undisturbed Portraits in Twilight

On walls hang pictures, faces stare,
With mustaches drawn, a comical affair.
One grins wide, a cake in hand,
While another waves from a slip and land.

Beneath the frames, shadows creep,
As secrets in the twilight seep.
Their giggles bounce from floor to beam,
In this gallery of a forgotten dream.

Faded Stories on Weathered Walls

The wallpaper peels with stories bright,
Of love and laughter, pure delight.
But oh, those stains from spilled tea cups,
Turned cloudy tales of friendship ups.

A ghost dog barks at the moonlit scene,
Chasing the echoes, unseen, serene.
While chairs creak under ancient spells,
In a symphony where history dwells.

Unraveled Dreams in the Parlor

A knitting basket with yarn gone wild,
Where socks are born, though none have smiled.
They plot escape, in tangled schemes,
A fuzzy caravan of woolly dreams.

The parlor clock ticks a funny beat,
As time confesses it's just a cheat.
With minutes lost to sleep and snacks,
Good friends and giggles fill the cracks.

Whispers in the Dust

In corners dark, the mice convene,
With whispers soft, they plot and scheme.
They giggle at the shoes left wide,
And dance beneath the couch with pride.

Each dust mote floats like tales untold,
Of sock puppets and ghosts that won't grow old.
They chuckle at the broom's despair,
While dust bunnies float up in the air.

Shadows of Silent Rooms

In a shadowy nook, a chair does squeak,
It tells silly tales, though few dare peak.
The curtains flutter, gossip they share,
Of crumbs and crumbs without a care.

A lamp flickers bright, with dreams of its own,
Wishing to trip on a cat or a bone.
All the while, walls listen and grin,
For shadows are secrets they keep within.

Memories Entwined in Silence

An old clock ticks, but it's out of time,
Waltzing to a rhythm that's quite a crime.
Dust falls like confetti from years gone by,
While a rubber duck watches with a sigh.

The fridge hums a tune of lost pizza slice,
While spoons laugh at forks for being so nice.
In every creak of the floor, there's a joke,
And the walls chuckle at secrets they poke.

The Voices We Left Behind

Forgotten shoes, they whisper and sway,
With anecdotes of laughter that faded away.
A voice from the closet starts to hum,
Reminiscing the days like a grumpy old drum.

The windows creak with tales of the past,
And floorboards giggle, it's all such a blast.
Echoes of pets, woofs, and meows,
Paint the air with joyous vows.

Reflections in Dusty Corners

In corners where dust bunnies play,
Squinty-eyed ghosts come out to say,
"Did we leave the light on in the past?"
"Or did we forget to have a blast?"

A sock's gone rogue, or so it seems,
Found a home in forgotten dreams.
A teacup giggles, its handle just right,
Sipping shadows, what a sight!

An old chair creaks a funny tune,
Chasing mice beneath the moon.
Whispers of laughter float through the air,
While tangled socks dance without a care.

The mirror reflects its own surprise,
As more than dust starts to arise.
With silly faces, the echoes play,
In corners where we laughed the day away.

The Lament of Lost Voices

Whispers of laughter hang like dust,
Piled high in corners, musty and rust.
Lost stories echo, each voice a jest,
Making memories in an echoing fest.

A shoe that squeaks has tales to tell,
Of journeys it took, of brief farewell.
It waltzes with dust in a cha-cha sway,
In the ballroom of silence, they secretly play.

Forgotten giggles in the lost and found,
As chairs hold court without a sound.
Dust motes dancing in the pale light glow,
Muffling laughter from long ago.

A curtain flutters, a shy little grin,
Inviting the echoes of chaos within.
Lost voices release their silent cheer,
As they tiptoe around, sneaky and clear.

Secret Chambers of Solitude

In secret rooms where shadows bloom,
Lonely knickknacks assume the gloom.
They swap old tales of the days gone by,
And tickle the dust while giggling shy.

A cat-shaped lamp snickers at night,
Sharing jokes with an old fruit bite.
Under the mattress, a pillow sighs,
Reacting to whispers from tired eyes.

Lamp post clinks as it leans to say,
"Solitude's fun in a quirky way!"
The echoing walls, they join in mirth,
As secrets find homes in their rebirth.

Unseen friend's banter, now loud and clear,
Echoes of joy waking up the drear.
In chambers of secrets, it's all quite neat,
With laughter hidden in every beat.

Stale Lullabies in Empty Rooms

In empty rooms with weary sighs,
A moth flits by, a wise disguise.
It croons stale songs to the cracked-up floors,
While dust bunnies dance through unlocked doors.

Cobwebs quiver in the moonlight glow,
Whispers exchanged between old and slow.
Lullabies given to the shadows round,
Where echoes of laughter almost found.

A forgotten teapot starts to whirr,
Sipping tea with a fluffy fur.
Its fables steeped in forgotten time,
Spilling humor with every climb.

Drapes flutter out of boredom's reach,
Practicing their method of speech.
Once lively rooms repose in jest,
As stale lullabies become their quest.

Possibilities Linger in the Shadows

In corners dark, the whispers play,
Mice tell tales of yesterday.
A sock's escape, a shoe's retreat,
All the odds and ends compete.

The shadows dance with ghostly glee,
A cat debates on climbing a tree.
Each squeak, a riddle, each laugh, a jest,
Life's nonsense is at its best.

The lightbulb flickers, a strobe of fun,
While dust bunnies spin, they've just begun.
Lost in the chaos, nothing feels wrong,
Like singing a silly, forgotten song.

Memories Cradled in the Walls

Inside the plaster, secrets leak,
Behind the paint, a puppy's peek.
A family feast turned into a fight,
The pie flew high, oh what a sight!

Chairs creak tales of raucous cheer,
And who forgot last year's souvenir?
The wallpaper sighs, its patterns swirl,
As socks grow legs and begin to twirl.

Echoes of laughter bounce in retro style,
Where grandma's stories go on for a while.
With each new dent, a story is told,
In this house of mischief, life never grows cold.

The Last Resonance of Farewell

A door slammed shut with a comic bang,
As grandma's cat let out a clang.
The dust motes danced in the final light,
As laughter faded into the night.

With each goodbye, a sock takes flight,
The fridge hums tunes that feel just right.
"Did we forget the cake?" someone yelled,
"Who left the pudding out?" everyone felled.

Echoes of joy in parting's embrace,
A squirrel that stole the last piece of grace.
Laughter lingers as shadows swirl,
In memories sweet, our hearts unfurl.

Echoes Between Here and Now

In the hallway, whispers tease,
A chortle here, a giggle, please!
A tuba's honk from the attic above,
Reminds us of the silly love.

Footsteps shuffle, a dance that's clumsy,
While spiders play tunes—aren't they so funny?
The echoes mingle, a canvas of cheer,
Mixing the past with all we hold dear.

Tick-tock, the clock knows every rhyme,
A cat prepares for a jump in time.
From giggles to sighs, the house wears a grin,
In echoes of joy, our tales begin.

Resonance of the Unseen

In corners hide the ghosts' delight,
With socks and shoes that took to flight.
They dance around, quite out of sight,
Telling tales of the past at night.

Old chairs creak as if to laugh,
While dishes argue over math.
A cat appears, it plays the staff,
And sings of hats that went in half.

Lamps flicker on a whim or two,
As shadows paint the walls anew.
What secrets lie in dust and glue,
Or marshmallow hearts that once flew?

In this abode of winks and grins,
A record spins, where madness wins.
Forget the dust, just count your sins,
As echoes cheer and life begins.

Whispers in the Attic

Up in the attic, a mouse plays chess,
With dust bunnies dressed in old dress.
They giggle softly, that charming mess,
While cobwebs weave a lace of stress.

The books have voices, full of puns,
Telling tales of their wild runs.
A rocking chair joins in the fun,
As time ticks on, no need to shun.

Beneath the beams, a gnome can skate,
Sliding around on piles of fate.
The air smells strange, a pie on plate,
While shadows join in to celebrate.

Oh, what a laugh, this place to roam,
With every squeak a joyful poem.
In playful whispers, we call it home,
Where lost things gather to freely comb.

Shadows of Silent Memories

In corners lurk the silly shades,
Hiding behind the old charades.
They chuckle at the joke cascades,
As time with laughter swiftly fades.

A pot of stew starts to arise,
With flavors full of weird surprise.
The kitchen sings with old goodbyes,
As echoes nibble on the pies.

A squirrel narrates the tales of old,
Of robots wearing hats of gold.
Each shadow giggles, bold yet cold,
Reminding all of stories told.

From ceiling cracks the laughter rains,
As unseen friends play funny games.
And though we can't recall their names,
Their playful echoes forge the flames.

Ghosts of a Time Unspoken

In the hallway, phantoms joke and jive,
With lightbulbs flickering, they're alive.
They trade old quips, give high fives,
While old clocks chime like bees in hives.

A sandwich laughs, it's quite absurd,
With mustard jokes and pickle words.
The wallpaper has memory blurred,
Of family jokes that feel inferred.

Ghostly pets wag their tails in fun,
Chasing after beams of morning sun.
With every pounce, they've just begun,
To dance and frolic, everyone!

So take a peek where shadows play,
In every nook, a bright bouquet.
Those unseen friends come out to stay,
And turn the night into a day.

Almanac of Echoed Cries

In the corners, whispers dance,
Dusty notes of a missed romance.
Loud laughter from a chair so old,
Tales of socks that went uncontrolled.

Ghosts with mismatched shoes parade,
Tripping over memories they made.
Silly sounds of hiccuped past,
As echoes chase shadows quite fast.

In the attic, a parrot sings,
Replaying all the silly things.
Jokes and jests from long ago,
In a symphony of remember-woe.

Yet laughter lingers, bright and spry,
As the echoes just can't say goodbye.
With every creak of weary wood,
They giggle softly, misunderstood.

Remnants of Heartbeats Past

A heartbeat echoes through the hall,
Was that a laugh or a friendly squall?
Each thud and bump, a comical spree,
Stumbling like an unwelcome bee.

Old chairs keep secrets, soft and snug,
While light bulbs flicker, giving a shrug.
Emotions bottled, then sadly spilled,
Craving punchlines that fate has killed.

Tick-tock clocks join in the fun,
Counting giggles till the day is done.
Forgotten hopes in paint-splattered frames,
All waiting here, just playing games.

Yet somehow, it feels like a show,
Where every flub is a chance to grow.
Though heartbeats fade, they keep the beat,
Turning echoes into laughter sweet.

Murmurs Behind Locked Doors

Behind the door, a whisper spills,
A pancake recipe chasing thrills.
Fried in laughter, turned in jest,
As echoes wake their morning quest.

Socks in hand, they tiptoe about,
Seeking the truth, then bursting out.
A secret dance, a noodle twirl,
As echoes spin and begin to whirl.

The mirror chuckles at the sight,
Of mismatched socks and socks of light.
Peeking through the cracks so wide,
Echoes seem to thrive inside.

Songs of chaos in each room,
Telling tales of impending doom.
Yet with each twist and turn we take,
The echoes giggle and hearts awake.

Ink Stains of Untold Stories

In an ink-splattered corner, tales reside,
Each story scribbled, hard to hide.
Doodle dreams of kittens and cheer,
Awake and echoing, loud and near.

A quill once dipped in laughter's well,
Dances across pages, sweet farewell.
The poet's block plays a prank or two,
Creating lines that just won't do.

Every dot a giggle, every swirl a sigh,
Mismatched words seem to fly high.
Yet below the garbled paper trail,
Are echoes of laughter that won't pale.

With each blotted story, a chuckle shines,
Footnotes of folly in quirky designs.
As ink flows erratic, wild and free,
Echoes emerge, crafting comedy.

Lament of the Unheard

In corners where the shadows lie,
Whispers bounce, but no one's nigh.
I talk to socks and chairs with glee,
   They nod along, but never see.

I staged a play with dust and dirt,
The audience tried to mutter, flirt.
But all they did was sit and stare,
I'm left to perform with empty air.

The fridge hums jokes that never land,
While my goldfish is my biggest fan.
He splashes laughter at every pun,
   But it's only me, the lonely one.

So here I dance, a silly mime,
To echoes that won't share a rhyme.
A one-man show in this old den,
Where laughter died — 'til I see them again.

Silence Paints the Walls

The wallpaper's peels, a hiding place,
For giggles caught in a silent race.
They painted whispers in shades of blue,
While I play host to the wild undo.

A chair with four legs, but only three dance,
It twirls on a whim, not leaving a chance.
The table's tickled by a passing breeze,
It chuckles softly, if you please!

I drape a shadow over the light,
It laughs back hungrily, teasing the night.
The clock ticks jokes like a comedian's shot,
Though the punchline's lost — er, maybe not!

So, join the chatter of things in this room,
Listen close, feel the laughter zoom.
In silence we paint a goofy spree,
Where echoes rustle — take a jab at me!

Portraits of Time and Memory

Framed on the walls, a grinning cat,
With a monocle, he looks just splat.
A portrait hung from the days of yore,
His whiskers twitch as old tales soar.

There's a snapshot of long-lost shoes,
They danced all night, but now they snooze.
Their formal wear is dusty and old,
Yet they recall a story brightly told.

A picture of me, with cake on my nose,
It captured a moment, who really knows?
The laughter echoes as I pout and grin,
In this gallery where memories spin.

Time is a jester, painting with glee,
Mocking the past in a whimsical spree.
Each laugh a stroke, each sigh a frame,
Here, in this hall, it's all a game!

The Attic's Dusty Promises

Up in the attic where dreams forget,
Dust bunnies plan their own minuet.
They twirl and leap, those fluff balls of cheer,
Making a mess as they disappear.

Old trunks sigh with the weight of time,
Hiding secrets in accordion rhyme.
They promise treasures wrapped tight in dust,
While I unwrap laughter that's a must!

A rocking horse waits for a gal to mount,
While the moths hold court, and all laugh, count!
There's magic here beneath the shrouds,
Where giggles surface and joy enclouds.

So climb the stairs, let the echoes play,
In the attic's corners, memories sway.
Promising dust-clouded smiles on each path,
Join the fun, and let's share a laugh!

Laughter Trails of Abandoned Spaces

In a room where no one stays,
Echoes dance and skip like rays.
A cat laughs at the dust on the floor,
While shadows giggle, wanting more.

A chair creaks with a ghostly sigh,
It remembers fun, oh my, oh my!
The fridge hums a vintage tune,
As spoons clatter, they join the croon.

Unseen guests at the coffee bar,
Debating if they'll take up a jar.
A humor lost in cobwebs and beams,
Sprinkling joy like glitter in dreams.

So raise a toast to the empty cheer,
For in silence, laughter's still near.
In corners where silliness thrives,
Abandoned spaces still feel alive.

The Pulse of an Emptied Home

A clock ticks loud, but nobody's here,
It keeps the time, devoid of fear.
Walls whisper jokes that no one hears,
While chairs reminisce on forgotten cheers.

The kitchen's secrets, a recipe lost,
Dancing pots, they laugh at the cost.
An empty chorus sings of delight,
As the dust bunnies take off in flight.

Creaky floorboards join in the fun,
With every step, a new pun is spun.
Behind the fridge, a sock comes to play,
Bidding farewell to a dreary day.

In this abode where silence can roam,
The pulse of jest beats on its own.
From cobwebs to rays of sunlight's grace,
This empty haven is a funny place.

Time's Whisper on Abandoned Stairs

Stairs groan with tales of days gone by,
Each step's a giggle, oh my, oh my!
Dusty boots with stories untold,
Chasing memories that never grow old.

The banister chuckles, a slippery tale,
Of a cat that forgot how to sail.
Down the steps, with a skip and a hop,
It rolled to the bottom, a comedy flop!

An old light bulb flickers with glee,
Casting shadows of people who once would be.
A coat rack leans, trying to stand tall,
While hats fall off, causing a sprawl.

With every creak, these stairs join in,
In a world of laughter, they spin and spin.
In forgotten corners, life softly dwells,
As time giggles under its whimsical spells.

Requiem of Forgotten Dreams

Beneath the bed, a shoe falls asleep,
With dreams of races, oh very deep.
A teddy bear plans a comedy show,
While the lamp chuckles, "Oh, what a glow!"

Windows sigh with forgotten views,
Gazing at clouds in whimsical hues.
An umbrella thinks it's a bird taking flight,
Swaying with laughter in the moonlight.

A drawer creaks, telling old tales,
Of socks mischief and lost mail trails.
With every sigh, the past takes a bow,
As laughter echoes, still lingering now.

In this soft requiem of whimsy and jest,
Forgotten dreams are still feeling blessed.
For in the quiet, their giggles hum,
In corners where laughter forever will come.

Lullabies of Echoing Silence

In corners where the dust bunnies roam,
A serenade hums, a child's wayward tome.
The creaky floors dance, in shoes made of cheese,
While shadows chuckle, in rustling leaves.

Whispers of giggles bounce off the walls,
As pillows conspire in whimsical brawls.
Lamps flicker glances, as secrets they keep,
Echoes retreat, just as we all sleep.

Lanterns for a Lost Heart

A lantern blinks, with a wink and a glow,
Chasing after shadows, that shuffle just so.
It trips on laughter, spills dreams on the floor,
With each little flicker, it giggles and roars.

The cobwebs tangle, like spaghetti in air,
As old socks rattle, with none left to care.
Spoons start a waltz, in the sink's silver stream,
While glasses laugh softly, lost in a dream.

Tapestry of Faded Joy

A tapestry hangs, stitched with delight,
Each thread a tale, in the soft morning light.
Buttons that jive, and ribbons that twirl,
Old pictures flutter, with a giggling swirl.

Chairs join the party, with squeaky applause,
In worn-out havens, where silence withdraws.
The clock shrugs its arms, with no care for the time,
As memories tiptoe, in an offbeat rhyme.

The Forgotten Harmonies of Home

A tune hums softly, from beneath the stair,
With spoons playing melodies, just floating in air.
Dust motes perform, in a sparkling ballet,
As chairs roll their eyes at the sounds of the day.

Clocks tick in chuckles, watches crack jokes,
While brooms break into laughter, in swirls and pokes.
Walls sigh with glee at the chaos they've seen,
As echoes wrap all in a sweet, silly sheen.

The Memory's Fading Song

In the attic, socks form a choir,
Worn-out sneakers fight like a tire.
Old ghosts dance in their favorite tune,
While the cat plays judge, a silent cartoon.

Dust bunnies wobble, taking a bow,
As creaky floorboards take their vow.
Chairs with wheels spin tales of woe,
Of picnics that vanished and socks that won't glow.

A treasure chest filled with lost advice,
Here lies a note: 'Don't eat cold rice!'
The clock ticks funny, it tells silly jokes,
While the fridge hums tunes from old vinyl folks.

In corners, the laundry holds its breath,
Whispers of socks that danced with death.
Yet laughter echoes, soft and profound,
In this quirky hall where oddities abound.

Haunted Reflections in Glass

Mirrors giggle at the faces they saw,
While my hair rebels, in total law.
Old friends caught in a dusty frame,
Grinning wide, oh what a game!

The vase hums tunes from floral days,
While forks debate the best food craze.
Chandeliers wink at passing guests,
Saying, 'We've outlasted all the tests!'

Socks argue over mismatched pairs,
Whispers of secrets in the cushioned chairs.
Even the walls roll their eyes in delight,
As memories dance through day and night.

Laughter sneezes from a dusty tome,
It finds a way to feel right at home.
The sneaky echoes, a cheeky crew,
In the playful haunt, we all outgrew.

Unseen Hands of Memory

Unseen hands play with forgotten toys,
Creating chaos with giggling noise.
In the corner, a bear gives a wink,
As mismatched socks plot the ultimate stink.

Old board games whisper forgotten rules,
While dolls engage in ridiculous duels.
A mirror catches a wink from a shoe,
Saying, 'You can't catch me, but I'll catch you!'

Ghostly whispers ride the breeze,
Tickling eardrums with playful tease.
A phantom cat chases a feather,
Turning old worries into silly tether.

Cobbwebs weave ridiculous tales,
Of where old toys set their sails.
In this romp, the past is unsealed,
With every chuckle, a memory revealed.

The Weight of Unheard Laughter

In quiet corners, giggles grow bold,
Whispers of stories left untold.
The curtains sway like they're in on the fun,
Fueled by shadows that laugh in the sun.

A missed tickle here, a silent shout,
Echoes of laughter that flit about.
Old shoes gather dust, now deep in thought,
Remembering games that the children forgot.

The ceiling hums with jests long gone,
As echoes strut in their favorite song.
Ghosts mix punch at the old tea table,
Crafting a ruckus, so charmingly stable.

Footprints of laughter trail through the gloom,
While walls keep secrets with a silent boom.
In this merry mirth of ghosts that play,
Unheard giggles color the mundane gray.

The Sound of Absence in the Air

In corners where laughter used to bloom,
Now only echoes of a dust bunny's zoom.
The chairs sit still, in quiet conspire,
While shadows do a dance, with no one to inspire.

A cat in the window, donning a frown,
Watching the dust motes float slowly down.
It paws at the silence, a curious fate,
But even the goldfish seems to await.

The fridge hums a tune, a one-note choir,
While the clock ticks on, with no one to tire.
A pizza's long gone, lost under a lid,
It giggles with cheese, unseen, and now hid.

In every odd creak, a friend may reside,
With memories swirling, they all seem to bide.
So hush now and listen to what it suggests,
An encore of chuckles from who knows the rest.

Whispers Lost in Time's Embrace

In the attic where socks go to meet,
They converse with old shoes in a dance so sweet.
A clock from the '70s softly chimes,
Like it lost its rhythm but still has the rhymes.

Beneath the old bed, a monster must dwell,
Or perhaps it's just crumbs from last week's farewell.
The curtains are gossiping, sharing old tales,
Of fights over dishes and runaway snales.

The mirror reflects a grin, what a mess,
It holds all the secrets; you wouldn't guess.
A toothbrush debates with a spatula's pride,
Together they ponder what dreams they have tried.

As shadows take shape, they form a parade,
Of laughter and whispers that fears have betrayed.
They leap like a dance, all free from despair,
In this refuge of nonsense, look beyond the glare.

Dusty Pages of a Forgotten Memoir

In the library's corner, a book's in a huff,
It grumbles about parties and not having enough.
Each page, a relic from days long past,
It chuckles and sneezes, its humor unsurpassed.

A dog-eared chapter on how to bake bread,
Might conspire with scones, leaving crumbs instead.
Ink blots play tag on the yellowing sheets,
While the tale of a cat names the strangest feats.

The writer once proud, with a well-inked pen,
Now wishes for tea and a raucous win again.
What fun can be found in the stories gone wild,
Where giggles of authors fill each passing child.

So linger a while, let the laughter ignite,
Among dusty collections, reimagine the flight.
For each jumbled word has a wink and a nod,
In this whimsical world, playfully flawed.

Secrets in the Crevices

In the crack by the door, a rumor takes flight,
Of lost left socks and epic pillow fights.
They whisper their tales of adventures so grand,
While lurking beneath is a sneaky dust band.

The walls hold their breath, with secrets to share,
Of echoes long gone, but laughter's still there.
A spider spins webs with a sly little grin,
Reciting old stories of what's been and when.

A mouse in the pantry writes memoirs of cheese,
Dreaming of life in seven different keys.
Each nibble a tale, each bite a new plot,
As cookies grow fonder of this curious lot.

In every tiny corner, a chuckle unfolds,
With whispers of warmth, as the universe molds.
Secrets remain, in the quirkiest flair,
Where silence and fun dance freely in air.

Resounding Silence of Past Homecomings

In the corner, a cat took a leap,
Chasing shadows, making a sweep.
Dust bunnies dance with a chuckle loud,
While Grandma's knitting makes me proud.

Forgotten chairs creak, tell old tales,
Of mishaps, mischief, and lost snail trails.
Each corner whispers in playful jest,
Of socks that wandered, a pesky quest.

The fridge hums tunes of leftovers past,
In a symphony deep, but not meant to last.
Timmy's first steps echoed down the hall,
With laughter, we stumbled, nearly took a fall.

So let's toast to echoes, both wild and tame,
To memories giggling, with no one to blame.
In this quirky realm where whispers play,
The resounding silence makes for a fun day.

Soft Cries in the Midnight Hour

Underneath stars, a ghostly wail,
Turns out to be a cat's midnight trail.
The fridge squeaks softly, like a little mouse,
While sleepwalking dogs roam through the house.

Whispers of dreams waft through the air,
As socks have discussions, without a care.
The clock ticks loudly, a comedic sound,
Of moments forgotten, yet here still found.

Under blankets, we stifle our giggles,
As shadows dance with the brightest of wiggles.
A plate once full now begs for a snack,
Echoes of feasting come creeping back.

So hush, little voices, let laughter reign,
In the soft-echoing hours, there's no such pain.
The cries are just echoes of joy long gone,
Where midnight capers play their sweet song.

Lighthouses of Echoed Longing

In a hallway where whispers collide,
Old toys plot mischief, heads held with pride.
Lighthouses flicker in forgotten light,
Guiding lost socks on their daring flight.

Pillow forts stand like castles grand,
Where dreams are castles built on sand.
With echoes of laughter that light up the night,
Even the rug starts to dance with delight.

The kitchen hums with nostalgia and cheer,
As we reminisce with each clatter near.
Flavors of childhood, a toast to the past,
With each echoed moment, the joy will last.

So gather the stories, the goofy and bright,
In the lighthouse of memories shining so light.
For joy isn't lost, it just chooses to dance,
In the echoes of longing, we take a chance.

Missed Moments in the Hall of Time

In a hall where time sometimes forgets,
Misplaced agendas and feline pets.
The echoes of laughter bounce off the walls,
As we trip on memories and dance through the halls.

Old pictures hang with a wink and a grin,
Once vibrant moments where chaos begins.
A tickle of laughter, a snort, and a sigh,
The ghost of a moment wanders on by.

In slippers of dreams, we stumble and slide,
Down the pathways of what we can't hide.
Ticking clocks laugh, they don't care for the grind,
In this hall of missed moments, joy's well-defined.

So raise a glass to the time that we keep,
In halls where laughter never knows sleep.
Though echoes may whisper of times we forget,
Each missed moment's a giggle, the best one yet.

Chasing the Faintest Echo

In halls where shadows dance and sway,
I hear a giggle from yesterday.
Is it the cat? Or just my mind?
Chasing whispers, I'm in a bind.

The fridge hums tunes from times of old,
As I recount stories, loud and bold.
Each creak's a chorus, each sigh's a song,
What's right is wrong, and what's wrong feels strong.

There's laughter trapped within the walls,
Bouncing back like rubber balls.
I swear I found my socks in there,
But they just disappeared in thin air!

So here I stand in this funny space,
Chasing sounds that quicken my pace.
How did I end up in this show?
Guess I'll just laugh and see where it goes!

Memories Beneath the Floorboards

Oh, what's that noise, a little squeak?
Beneath my feet, the past does speak.
Maybe it's a mouse with a tale to tell,
Or old sock puppets stuck in a spell!

I find candy wrappers from times of glee,
Were they mine, or did ghosts have a spree?
Each crunching echo makes me pause,
Reminds me of snacks without a cause.

There's a snicker there, beneath the wood,
Are ghosts judging me? They probably should!
But as they giggle at my clumsy stance,
I can't help but join in their silly dance.

Dust bunnies whisper secrets and lore,
Regaling me with tales of yore.
I'll never run from the bobbles and nods,
Here's to memories beneath the odds!

Haunting Footsteps in the Hallway

Tipsy toes on creaky floors,
Are those footsteps or open doors?
I tiptoe in with a nervous grin,
But the sound just giggles and reels me in.

Every night, that patter starts,
A spectral dance of foolish arts.
I'll serve them tea and beg for dance,
They took my heart, should I take a chance?

Broomsticks bump in fits of glee,
They lead me on through rooms carefree.
Is that the ghost of Auntie Sue?
Or just me tumbling on a shoe?

In a case of mistaken fright,
We dance 'til dawn, what a sight!
So when you hear those playful feet,
Join the fun, it's quite a treat!

Threads of Past Conversations

Underneath the dusty beams,
Echoes weave their funny schemes.
I catch the chatter of days gone by,
Like two old socks in a pie in the sky!

Did Granny say to wash the cat?
Or was it Uncle Joe's smelly hat?
A jumble of voices fills the air,
While I sit puzzled, trying to compare.

Each thread pulls tight like a crazy quilt,
Fables of laughter and tales of guilt.
I listen close, the stories blend,
It's a slumber party, never end!

So if you find the threads unwind,
Know it's just the laughs they left behind.
Join the echoes, don't take fright,
You might just find pure delight!

Songs of Yesteryear's Twilight

In the attic, hats stacked high,
A tap-dancing dog caught the eye.
He waltzed with a broom, what a sight!
Echoes of laughter filled the night.

Old records spin, crackle away,
A ghost in a tux thinks it's ballet.
He trips on a rug, what a blunder!
It's funny how memories chase like thunder.

Dust bunnies leap like ballerina dreams,
While shadows play tricks in moonlit streams.
Grandma's old chair creaks as it grins,
Pretending to listen to old violin spins.

Each note a chuckle, each pause a tease,
In a symphony of slips and wheezes.
The twilight sings, with a twinkle and chime,
As echoes of yesteryear dance in rhyme.

Cracked Mirrors of Reflection

Mirrors cracked with a grin so wide,
Show funny faces, nowhere to hide.
Laughter erupts at the silly sight,
Reflections of joy in the pale moonlight.

A cat wearing glasses reads the news,
Sipping hot cocoa and sporting big shoes.
Next to him, a chicken struts proud,
Bok-bok-ing tales to an invisible crowd.

Scholars ponder, pondering away,
While clowns with canes play in dismay.
What wisdom they share in their zany spree,
Funny how truth can twist whimsically.

In shattered glass, we see our past,
Through humor and laughter, joy is cast.
Life's a circus, funny and bright,
In the cracked mirrors, we find delight.

Fractured Time in Shadowed Halls

Tick-tock, the clock takes a leap,
While turtles race and rabbits sleep.
A snail runs a marathon, how absurd,
Time shatters as laughter is heard.

Puppets dance in the dim-lit space,
Making faces, an unruly grace.
Each tick of the clock makes a jest,
Fractured time puts humor to the test.

Ghosts play cards with mischievous flair,
Shuffling the deck without a care.
An echo remarks, "What's the score?"
Laughter erupts, "I win once more!"

In shadowed halls, time's all askew,
Moments are silly, never quite true.
With each fractured tick, joy intertwines,
In each bend of time, laughter shines.

The Echoing Void of What Was

In a hall where echoes stumble and fall,
A jester appears, sporting a sprawl.
He spins tales of blunders, big and small,
In the echoing void, laughter befalls.

Old chairs gossip, sharing their woes,
About the socks lost in laundry flows.
An out-of-tune piano tries to sing,
With every note, a chuckle it brings.

Photographs wave with a wink and a grin,
Reminiscing about the mischief within.
They tell of the times when they were the best,
In the void of memories that never rest.

So join the feast of the echoes so clear,
As folly and fun bring the past near.
In timeless laughter, forever we'll be,
In the echoing void, just you and me.

Half-Remembered Dreams in the Dawn

In the early light, they dance,
Jumpy shadows with a chance.
Coffee cups do a little jig,
While toast sings a poppy gig.

Socks seem lost, a wild affair,
One left here, the other rare.
The fridge hums a sleepy tune,
As spoons gossip with a swoon.

Chairs whisper tales of night's surprise,
Napping cats with glowing eyes.
The clock ticks time with silly flair,
Counting dreams as if they dare.

Rug's a circus of sneaky crumbs,
Bouncing 'round like little drums.
In this dawn, laughter flows free,
Half-remembered, yet so key.

Muffled Conversations in Dusty Air

Whispers glide on cobweb strands,
Broomsticks holding up their hands.
Dust motes dance, a waltzy breeze,
While books chuckle atop their fleas.

Once upon a wall, it sighed,
Framed in laughter, though it tried.
Mice check in at the old fridge door,
Offering crumbs and wanting more.

Peeking curtains, what a joke,
Watching with an old, dry poke.
Radio static joins the fun,
Telling secrets from everyone.

Echoes tickle every nook,
A silent giggle, a friendly cook.
In this air, the jokes run deep,
Muffled, funny, in dreams we keep.

The Essence of Forgotten Footprints

Footprints made of laughter bright,
Lead to corners, out of sight.
Squeaky shoes on echo's trace,
Start a dance, leave no base.

Puddle jumps with silly glee,
Splashing tales from you to me.
An ice cream cone that took a dive,
Yells, 'Come back! I'm still alive!'

Paths of giggles crisscross round,
In silly shapes, they're bounce-bound.
Funky socks and mismatched shoes,
Live in stories we choose to choose.

Laughter plastered on the wall,
With sketched-out wishes, we enthrall.
In the essence of lost run,
We find the joy of silly fun.

Breaths of Yesterday's Passion

Whisking flour, there's a plot,
Cookies bear a battle spot.
In the oven, they conspire,
To rise up in hilarious fire.

Yesterday's fun in the air,
A cat plays tag with a chair.
Whiskers twitching, such a dance,
While the dog beeps at every chance.

Banana peels spread wide and bright,
Slipping up the morning light.
Songs of laughter in every room,
Breathing life into the gloom.

In the remnants, joy takes flight,
In every giggle, love feels right.
Yesterday's passion transforms anew,
With every breath, it feels like glue.

Sighs of the Absent

In corners where dust bunnies prance,
Cozy chairs hold an old romance.
Creaking floors sing a silly tune,
While socks hide away, under the moon.

Jars of jam once danced with delight,
Now squished in the fridge, out of sight.
Every whisper of an empty hall,
Recalls a party that never was it all!

Potatoes laugh in the pantry's shade,
Comics piled high, slowly fade.
The cat pretends to be on a quest,
While it naps on the couch, quite at rest.

Imagine the echo of laughter here,
From voices we loved, now just a cheer.
Each memory's a jest, played too loud,
In the silence, we form quite the crowd.

Narrative Fragments Beneath the Eaves

Under beams that wobble and sway,
Old tales spin in a comical way.
A dust mote winks, saying, 'Hello,'
As stories meander, where did they go?

Books piled high, with covers that grin,
Age-old secrets hidden within.
A pair of shoes, mismatched, they tease,
Whispers of journeys lost in the breeze.

Ghostly giggles escape from the floor,
Echoing softly like never before.
The lamp has tales of a lighthearted muse,
Was it a ghost or just a ruse?

From empty rooms where echoes collide,
Laughter's quick twist, it tries to hide.
And every crack tells of ages gone by,
While we laugh at the mischief, not asking why.

Abandoned Games and Silent Laughter

In the attic where shadows play tag,
Forgotten toys rest, a weary rag.
Dolls with hair, half out of place,
Bringing squeals from a lost embrace.

Cards shuffled once near the window pane,
Left to weather a gentle rain.
Marbles roll free, under the couch,
While laughter echoes, a cheeky vouch.

The board game waits with a cheeky smirk,
Hoping for players to join in the perk.
While dice tumble down, they giggle without end,
A reminder that all things can bend.

Unruly hats hang by the door,
The merry spirits still yearn to explore.
In every corner, a chuckle takes flight,
As memories rattle, bringing delight.

Traces of Joy in the Erosion of Time

Rusty toys left to glimmer and rust,
Remembering joys that went with a gust.
Every crevice is filled with glee,
While the clock ticks softly, counting with me.

Footprints of laughter trail through the hall,
Lingering shadows, like an old ball.
A cat's soft purr is a jolly refrain,
As it curates memories that still remain.

Colors fade but the smiles stay bright,
In corners where day spills into night.
Chairs gather dust yet still seem to cheer,
While tales of fun float softly near.

As time passes on with a quirky style,
Echoes remind us of every small smile.
So we'll gather here, as we always do,
In the laughter of echoes, that still feel new.

Ghosts of Laughter and Tears

In shadows where the chuckles dwell,
A poltergeist cracks jokes quite well.
With every creak, a laugh resounds,
Spinning tales amongst the mounds.

Oh, the specters in silly hats,
Doing the moonwalk with house cats.
They dance about in playful binds,
Wrapping glee in tangled minds.

But don't be fooled by ghostly cheer,
For haunted pranks bring up a sneer.
With whoopee cushions, they employ,
A spectral touch of silly joy.

Yet amidst the laughter, droplets flow,
An echoing tale of woe below.
Teardrops mix with giggles tight,
In the crypt where joy meets fright.

Chasing Faint Reverberations

Faint whispers echo down the hall,
A chorus of giggles begins to sprawl.
The walls chuckle with every creak,
As echoes dance, hide and seek.

With every ghostly shout and cheer,
The laughter pulls you ever near.
Chasing sounds that fade away,
While shadows join the fun to play.

Footsteps stumble on the floor,
As phantoms giggle, ask for more.
They throw a party, just their kind,
With snacks that disappear, confined.

So come and join this spectral spree,
Dodge the whispers, set them free!
For in the echo, joy collides,
A riot of laughter, where hope abides.

Crumbling Walls of Lost Dreams

The walls may sag and paint may peel,
But dreams of laughter always heal.
With every crack, a story formed,
Of joy and pranks, where all was warmed.

There once lived a cat who told old jokes,
While other ghosts had brunch with folks.
Crumbling tiles beneath their feet,
They danced in a rhythm, oh so sweet.

The ceiling fans whirl a tale so absurd,
Of flying pies and dancing birds.
As laughter echoes in each small room,
Bringing life to the gathering gloom.

Still, dreams collapse with each hoot and shout,
While giggling ghosts rush in and out.
In this place where echoes stay,
Joy lingers on, come what may.

The Language of Forgotten Places

In cobwebbed corners, whispers play,
A silly language leads the way.
With chuckles soaring through the air,
Forgotten tales begin to share.

Ghosts conduct a symphony grand,
Of laughter echoing, hand in hand.
They speak in giggles, wrapped in glee,
A pun-filled world where all are free.

They mime out scenes, absurd and bright,
While shadows twirl in joyous flight.
A waltz of echoes, weird and fun,
In this domain, all burdens shun.

So gather round, and lend an ear,
To the melodies that tickle near.
For in these halls of lost old traces,
Laughter blooms, in forgotten places.

Ghostly Laughter in Abandoned Spaces

In a dusty room, a chair did squeak,
A ghostly giggle, so loud yet meek.
Old shoes tap dance on the wooden floor,
Who knew spirits could love to explore?

Cobwebs draped like fancy gowns,
While shadows weave their silly frowns.
Chattering critters, a raucous affair,
Echo through halls with a laugh to share.

A cloaked figure slipped on a banana peel,
"Oh my! How clumsy! I cannot conceal!"
With laughter ringing, they vanish like smoke,
What a surprise for the next sleepy bloke!

So next time you wander through an old, creaky door,
Listen for chuckles; there's fun to explore.
For even in silence, the giggles collide,
In a realm full of wonders where laughter won't hide.

Echoes of Joy in Sorrowful Places

In shadows deep where sorrows dwell,
A quirky note breaks the sorrowful spell.
A phantom jumps and performs a jig,
With a wink and a nod, they dance quite big.

Cracked mirrors reflect playful grins,
While memories hum off-key violin spins.
Old stories chuckle, long forgotten lore,
As echoes of joy bounce from wall to floor.

A lonely bench where dreams went to nap,
Springs up to life with a snazzy clap!
"Here's to the past, let's give it a twist,
A toast to the fun that we can't resist!"

So tiptoe lightly through places of gray,
For laughter can light up the saddest day.
In the corners where sighs seem to linger,
You might find a giggle that tickles your finger.

The Last Light of Forgotten Days

As twilight tucks in all the lost dreams,
The last light flickers, a wink that beams.
Old toys whisper secrets, lost in a race,
While shadows chase laughter around the place.

In shelves of dust, a tin can rolls free,
"Catch me if you can!" calls a quirky bee.
The moon takes a bow, the stars start to glow,
Laughter echoes softly where no one will go.

A clock stuck at noon begins to chime,
"Let's dance through the hours, it's the silliest time!"
Forgotten delights chuckle in the night,
As the last light winks with sheer delight.

So linger a moment in whimsy's embrace,
Where memories playfully flaunt their grace.
In the glow of the dusk, join the revelry,
For even the past holds hilarity!

Relics of Lament in Quiet Nooks

In a corner nook where silence resides,
A teacup giggles, its laughter hides.
Dusty books wink, their stories untold,
While slippers scamper like they're bold.

A picture frame laughs at its crooked face,
As time marches by at a whimsical pace.
Memories chuckle in pinches and snorts,
Relics of sorrow now play their sports.

An old radio hums a funky tune,
Enticing the spirits to groovily swoon.
"Let's dance through the ages, bring out your flair,
In this quiet nook, you'll find laughter to share!"

So step into spaces where echoes collide,
With whispers of joy that long here abide.
For relics once mourned now sparkle and joke,
In corners where laughter beats even the smoke.

Echoes of Yesterday's Light

In the attic, spiders dance,
Dusty dreams take silly chance.
Old toys laugh, in shades of glee,
As echoes swing from tree to tree.

Laughter rings in empty halls,
Where mismatched socks bounce off the walls.
A cat that thinks it's king of all,
Snoozes soundly, no heed to the call.

A clock ticks wildly, out of time,
Tickling ears with silly chimes.
Ghosts in sheets play peekaboo,
While memories wave, 'Hello to you!'

Golden rays in pockets hide,
Mischievous thoughts that slip and slide.
Each shadow wears a jester's crown,
Making every frown turn upside down.

Faded Footsteps on Hollow Floors

Upon the stairs, a shuffle heard,
Echoes leap, without a word.
Old boots that tread on laughing wood,
Waltzing in a playful mood.

Mice with socks play hide and seek,
Rats in hats perform and squeak.
The floorboards creak, a voice they lend,
As every twist brings laughter's end.

Slippers with flapping, floppy ties,
Chase the dust clouds in wild flies.
The hallway giggles, walls resound,
With secrets that must not be found.

To the couch, the old cat glides,
Where the invisible humor hides.
Footsteps fade with each new dawn,
Yet the laughter lingers on.

Secrets Beneath the Stairway

Beneath the steps, a treasure trove,
Of mismatched socks and crumbs to rove.
Old secrets whisper in the gloom,
While raccoons plot to redecorate the room.

A rubber chicken finds some flair,
Sprouting feathers from thin air.
Ghostly giggles snicker, oh my!
As dusty old jokes dance on by.

Forgotten notes of love's sweet tease,
Wrapped in wrappers, swaying with ease.
The wooden beams are all in on it,
Joining in for a silly skit.

In corners dark, odd things reside,
Misfit toys on a jolly ride.
Each cranny hums a lively tune,
As shadows shimmy beneath the moon.

Reflections in Abandoned Mirrors

In mirrors cracked, the jesters play,
With funny faces on dismay.
Shadows stretch and giggle wide,
As silly laughs come out to hide.

A cat winks back with a grand pose,
While a ghostly friend chews on a rose.
Reflections dance in polka dots,
And conjure laughs from all the spots.

Old portraits grin, their eyes aglow,
Mimicking each silly show.
Tickled by time, they sway and spin,
With every glance, they invite you in.

Amongst the dust, humor lies,
In frames where laughter never dies.
So peek inside, and take a chance,
For every glance compels a dance.

Sunkissed Corners of Silent Affection

In corners where sunlight plays,
Dust bunnies dance in a haze,
The cat plots a sneaky attack,
While socks disappear, what a knack!

Cushions whisper secrets of yore,
As mittens argue on the floor,
A spoon takes a dive in the stew,
Who knew cookware could have a view?

The pet goldfish grins from its glass,
While crumbs plot a ninja-like pass,
With giggles that float through the air,
Each tickle of laughter is rare!

And in this nook of silent glee,
We craft our own quirky symphony,
Where echoes of chuckles convene,
In a world only we have seen!

Memories Whispered in the Wind

Whiskers twitch in the summer breeze,
A garden gnome holds his knees,
The wind carries tales, oh so bold,
Of yarn balls (and a sock theft) told!

The sunbeam flirts with the tile floor,
While a chair creaks, craving for more,
A cupboard with secrets unseen,
Hides leftovers of a dinner routine!

Windsurfing chairs race 'cross the room,
Bravely facing the dust bunny's gloom,
And every corner has something to share,
Like tales of a Thimble — or a lost pair!

With laughter echoing soft and slow,
We frolic where the old memories flow,
For even whispers can make you grin,
In this whimsical world, we swim!

The Quietude of Echoing Days

In a house that bumbles through time,
Where objects whisper in silly rhyme,
The fridge hums a tuneful refrain,
While the toaster dances, never plain!

The calendar hangs, its dates all a blur,
With notes from a pet that made us stir,
Who knew a paw could write such a tale,
Of late-night snacks that just went stale?

Chairs gossip about yesterday's feast,
While dust settles like a gentle beast,
And the rug bears the weight of our dreams,
Where laughter floats like cotton candy streams!

Through windowpanes, the world peeks in,
Drawing smiles from the chaos within,
A symphony of echoes and sighs,
Making mundane days wear surprise!

Timeless Stories in Faded Light

In twilight glow, shadows play tricks,
As bookshelves plot and pantry wicks,
A lamp flickers, barely awake,
While teacups gossip of joy and heartbreak!

Nostalgia hangs like an old coat,
With tales woven in every note,
A cupboard sighs, holding its breath,
Knowing secrets of laughter and death!

Every creak tells of unspoken days,
When life was a laugh, and silly ways,
From misplaced keys to lost teddy bears,
These echoes of joy are our timeless fare!

So gather 'round for a tale or two,
Where shadows dance, and giggles ensue,
In rooms where timeless stories ignite,
Faded light cradles delight!

Lingering Shadows of Yesterday

In corners where dust bunnies hide,
Laughter echoes, can't be denied.
A chair that creaks with a goofy grin,
Whispers of tales where we all fit in.

The sofa wears crumbs like a proud patch,
An old sock's love for a couch is a match.
Memories bounce like a rubber ball,
Reminding us, we had quite the fall.

Pictures with faces all out of line,
Each smile just a bit too divine.
They wink and nod, oh what a sight,
As we reminisce deep into the night.

So let's forget and just embrace,
The joyful rumble of this old place.
With laughter so loud it shakes the walls,
Echoes of fun in our silly brawls.

The Scent of Forgotten Affection

A whiff of cookies that once adorned,
The kitchen where sweet dreams were born.
But now it's just a place for dust,
And crumbs of love, oh how they rust.

Tupperware scattered like lost hopes,
Each lid missing, yet everyone copes.
Garlic leftover from a night of glee,
Whispers of romance, just wait and see.

Coffee mugs dance with ghostly cheer,
They clink and clatter as if to jeer.
A spoon with a story, a fork with a fate,
In this kitchen where laughter waits.

So raise a glass to the scents we cherish,
Even faded love, we'll never let perish.
For in every whiff lies a jest or two,
Reminding us of all we've been through.

Beneath the Weight of Unspoken Words

In a room where sighs seem to stack,
Whispers of chaos, oh, what a knack!
The cat meows secrets, her tale quite long,
While we trip over lines to which we belong.

Conversations linger like bad cologne,
Lost in translation, yet somehow we groan.
Old jokes resurface, a chuckle or two,
Beneath all the weight, we still break through.

Sticky notes scattered with thoughts quite bizarre,
Like "Clean the fridge" or "Tap dance on a star."
Each message a giggle, a beckon so sweet,
We stumble through life on our own two feet.

So let's dance with shadows, let gobbledygook reign,
For beneath the weight, we find the refrain.
With every chuckle, we conquer our fears,
And laugh 'til we cry through the unspoken years.

Quarters of Quiet Regret

In rooms where silence pretends to chat,
Regrets wear pajamas, how silly is that?
A lamp flickers strangely, like it wants to tell,
Of all the secrets it knows quite well.

A plant that's wilting holds its breath tight,
Wondering where all the love took flight.
An empty bowl that once held delight,
Now echoes with sounds of a long-lost bite.

Each chair sighs softly, a heart worn thin,
As we ponder the places we've never been.
The clock ticks loudly, in a comical show,
Time's just a jester, don't you know?

So let's toast to the echoes of things we regret,
In quarters so quiet, a laugh is our debt.
For from every moment, in jest we connect,
Even in silence, there's joy to collect.

www.ingramcontent.com/pod-product-compliance
Lightning Source LLC
Chambersburg PA
CBHW060142230426
43661CB00003B/530